for Today's Catholic

Beliefs, Practices, Prayers

Beliefs, Practices, Prayers

Neil Ormerod

A Division of HarperCollins*Publishers*

Published by Collins Dove
A Division of HarperCollins*Publishers* (Australia) Pty Ltd
22-24 Joseph Street
North Blackburn, Victoria 3130

First published 1992
Designed by William Hung
Cover design by William Hung
Cover photograph by Christine Ramsay

Typeset in Times by Collins Dove Desktop Typesetting
Printed in Australia by Griffin Press

The National Library of Australia
Cataloguing-in-Publication Data:

Ormerod, Neil.
A new handbook for today's Catholic.

ISBN 1 86371 129 5.

1. Catholic Church — Doctrines. 2. Catholic Church — Liturgy.
I. Title. (Series: Parish pamphlet series).

230.2

Nihil Obstat: Rev. Peter J. Kenny, D.D. Diocesan Censor
Imprimatur: Rev. Monsignor H.F. Deakin, Ph.D. Vicar General
Date: 25th March, 1992.

Acknowledgements
Our thanks go to those who have given us permission to reproduce copyright material in this book. Particular sources of print material are acknowledged in the text. Every effort has been made to contact the copyright holders of text material. The editor and publisher apologise in those cases where this has proven impossible.

Acknowledgements

I would like to take this opportunity to thank those who played a part in the writing of this booklet. Their many comments on early drafts of the text were invaluable to me in finalising my work - Paul Cashen MSC, Michael Fallon MSC, Philip Malone MSC, colleagues at St Paul's National Seminary Kensington; Fr John McSweeney, my parish priest at Kingsgrove; Mauro Di Nicola, senior school teacher and friend; John Collins, Catholic Adult Education, Sydney. My heartfelt thanks to them all.

I dedicate this book to Josey and all the searchers, and it is my hope that it will provide a clear, yet brief statement of the heart of Catholicism, as I have known and loved it.

Neil Ormerod

~

For Catholics, the most significant sign of the continued presence of Jesus in the world is in his eucharistic presence in the consecrated elements of bread and wine ....

~

Contents

Prayer

When you are praying, do not heap up empty phrases as the Gentiles do; for they think that they will be heard because of their many words. Do not be like them, for your Father knows what you need before you ask him. Pray then in this way: Our Father . . .

(Matthew 6:7-9)

Prayer as encounter with mystery

The starting point for all religious faith, and Catholic faith in particular, is the experience of a mystery at the heart of life. In the human heart we find a deep restlessness, a deep yearning to have and to be more. While society tells us that this can be fulfilled by owning and consuming more, such solutions do not diminish our restlessness. Indeed, they often make it more acute. Our restless heart pushes us not in the direction of more possessions, but in the direction of a greater wholeness, a greater integrity, a fulness of life welling up within. Our restless heart senses at the core of life a fullness of integrity, of goodness, which is not ours to command or control, but which beckons us forward and sustains us in our searching. In our searching we find symbols and words which seek to express this mystery which is beyond all symbols and words, but ultimately we must fall before this mystery in reverential awe, in silence and wonder. Such is the experience of prayer.

Christians name this mystery at the heart of life 'God'. God is the one who sustains and beckons us as we search for direction and meaning in the bustle of life. God is the still point in a turning world, the one reference point, the beacon which shows the way. In the course of our search, God draws us aside to refresh and sustain us, to challenge and confront us, to comfort and console us. At the centre of Christian faith lies the belief that this mystery we call God is Love - 'God is love' (I John 4:8) - a Love that knows no bounds, that embraces all, a Love in which there is no darkness. It is Love that sustains and beckons us, Love that invites us into the intimacy of prayer.

Prayer is not primarily something we do, some performance

we carry out. Most importantly, prayer is not some attempt to manipulate the mystery that is beyond all our powers to control. In prayer we acknowledge that we are not the centre, that we are not the conductor of the orchestra of life. Prayer is a response to an invitation, an invitation to a personal encounter with mystery. On our part, there is the need to make space, as St Augustine says a 'space for love to widen'. We need, at times, to withdraw from the bustle of life, to 'be still and know that I am God' (Psalm 46:10). But even in making such a space we are responding to an invitation, a beckoning, 'no one can come to me unless drawn by the Father'. (John 6:44)

There is no place for pretence in prayer. We cannot fool God. In prayer we come as we are, with all our faults and limitations, all our feelings of hurt and pain and anger, with all our hopes and disappointments. God knows all of these so there is no point in hiding them, or pretending they do not exist. Our honesty is not for God's sake, but for our own. Such honesty, such integrity is essential if we are not to lose direction. If we do not know where we are, we will never know where we are going! Indeed, in authentic prayer, God's promptings will force us to acknowledge things about ourselves we would rather not admit, things we don't even acknowledge. It is only by bringing such darkness into the light of God's love that we can experience true healing, and forgiveness for the many times we have lost our direction.

The key to prayer is simplicity. There can be no pretence, no deceit, no attempt to manipulate God, for God can see through it all. God simply asks us to be with God, to share in God's presence. This is God's most precious gift to us. Indeed, in some sense, prayer is a training in such simplicity. For when we bring such a simplicity to all we do, we have found our direction - 'Blessed are the pure in heart, for they will see God' (Matthew 5:8). The life of prayer gives a fruitful harvest of good works, so that 'they may see your good works and give glory to your Father in heaven' (Matthew 5:16). Then we can truly say that we pray always.

Prayer and prayers

Through the generations there have been men and women whose search for direction and meaning has brought them very close to the mystery we call God. With the simplicity that comes of prayer, these men and women have sought to express in words something of the spirit - the attitudes, the qualities, the dispositions - which has informed their own search. Such words, or prayers, are a pale reflection of a mystery which is beyond all words, yet in our human weakness, prayers can help us to focus our attention and give expression to our own unspoken yearnings. Prayers can be the first steps of prayer. They can help us draw together our hearts and minds to focus on the one essential matter - how we stand in relation to God.

While such prayers are the first steps in prayer, they can also be a distraction. Thus Jesus warned his disciples: 'When you are praying, do not heap up empty phrases as the Gentiles do; for they think that they will be heard because of their many words.' (Matthew 6:7)

The saying of 'many words' can betray a real anxiety. Many words can become a barrier between us and God, because, rather than approaching God in simplicity, we spend so much time and energy saying things that we forget to listen to God. Prayer can then become a pretence, an attempt to hide who I am. At the same time, I can feel self-righteous about having 'done a good thing'. Saying 'prayers' without the attitude of simplicity and openness is not real prayer at all. It does not create a space for love to widen, but encloses me in my anxieties, confirms me in my prejudices, hardens my heart.

Still, prayers remain an important part of the life of prayer. Jesus himself taught his disciples a prayer when they asked him: 'Lord teach us to pray' (Luke 11:1). This prayer, as recorded in Matthew's Gospel, is as follows:

Our Father in heaven,
hallowed be your name.
Your kingdom come.
Your will be done,
on earth as in heaven.
Give us this day our daily bread.
And forgive us our debts,
as we also have forgiven our debtors.
And do not bring us to the time of trial,
but rescue us from the evil one (Matthew 6: 9–13).

This prayer demonstrates the attitudes of simplicity and openness which are essential to authentic prayer. The immediate focus of the prayer is on God, the Father. God is the centre and source of our life. It is God's Kingdom, God's will, which provides direction and meaning. We stand before this holy mystery and open ourselves up in wonder and awe. In true acknowledgement of our total dependence on God, we ask for the most basic of necessities for human life - our daily bread. We recognise the times when we have lost our direction, and humbly ask for divine forgiveness. Yet we realise that the measure of our living is not found in some exclusive compartment called 'religion'. Rather, it is found in the human relationships which make up our life. Thus we cannot ask for more forgiveness than we have been willing to give to others. Indeed our unwillingness to forgive can close us off from being open to God's forgiveness. Finally, we address our greatest anxiety, the possibility of totally losing our direction, of being overwhelmed by the 'evil one'. Only God's sustaining love can save us from such a fate.

There are many other prayers which form part of the Christian and Catholic tradition. Some of these are recorded in an appendix to this booklet. The Psalms in the Bible are also part of this living tradition of prayer. All these have their place in the life of prayer and are an indispensable resource, but just as important are our own spontaneous prayers, the words and feelings which tumble out of us as we seek to give expression to where we are and how we feel at a particular moment in our life. Sometimes, the words of the mystics and saints, however sacred, do not express how I feel now, at this moment in time, with these particular anxieties and fears, joys and hopes. Only *I* can express this, only *I* can offer this at God's holy altar. Then I must speak, not with the words of others, but with my own, knowing that these are the most honest expression I can give to my life.

Of course, there are times when even this stream of words from the heart will fail to express all that I feel, all that I am. There are times when I feel overwhelmed, either by anxiety or awe, when no words are adequate, when words simply fail. Yet this does not put an end to prayer. As St Paul taught us:

> *Likewise the Spirit helps us in our weakness; for we do not know how to pray as we ought, but that very Spirit intercedes with sighs too deep for words. And God, who searches the heart, know what is the mind of the Spirit, because the Spirit intercedes for the saints according to the will of God* (Romans 8:26–27).

So we need never feel anxious when we can no longer find words to express our prayer. We can be confident that God hears the petitions made by the Spirit on our behalf.

Prayer as life

Prayer must become part of the rhythm of our lives. This does not mean that we have to spend a lot of time praying, or saying a lot of prayers. Rather, we need to become reflective people, reflecting on our lives, our relationships, our values, the direction in which our lives are heading. We need to take stock of ourselves constantly, so that when we do spend time in prayer, we are not strangers to ourselves.

Such a reflective attitude does not mean self-absorption, or self-consciousness. It is not a matter of endless self-analysis, of feeling guilty about the past or anxious about the future. Rather, it means developing a contemplative spirit. Then we become absorbed, not in our own worries and concerns, but in reality, the reality of our lives. How do we relate to those in our family, to friends or those we see as hostile towards us? How do we relate to the wider matters of life, to our society, to the global community? These are some of the elements that make up the reality of our lives and ultimately, it is through these that we relate to God. A contemplative spirit broadens our horizon so that we can see the fuller picture.

Indeed, prayer means letting go of *my* perspective, to see things from the perspective of God, to see the fuller picture. As people once saw the earth as the centre of the universe, so we all tend to see ourselves as the centre of the world. In prayer we re-centre our world on God. This attitude can then flow over into our living so that we can begin to see the real needs of those around us. When seen from God's perspective, these needs become an opportunity for us to share in God's saving work for others. Without this perspective, such needs are seen more as a threat to us, making demands we cannot fulfil.

Finally, we need to keep before us constantly the values of our religious tradition. For the Catholic this will mean a familiarity with the Scriptures, especially the Psalms and the Gospels, and the prayers of the liturgy. The parables and sayings of Jesus, particularly the Sermon on the Mount (Matthew 5–7), are a rich source of material for reflection leading into prayer. The more familiar we are with these, the more they will permeate our thinking and our decisions, and nourish our prayer. The briefest moment, recalling a saying of Jesus as applicable to me here and now, for example, can be a moment of intense prayer.

In all these ways, prayer can become part of the rhythm of my life. In as much as this happens we can see noticeable effects on the quality of our living. We become changed people. We begin to reflect more of what St Paul calls the fruits of the Spirit - 'love, joy, peace, patience, kindness, generosity, faithfulness, gentleness and self-control' (Galatians 5:22–23). These fruits provide a real touchstone for our growth in the life of prayer.

Liturgy and public prayer

While prayer is intensely personal, the realism of prayer demands that we recognise that the same search for direction is going on all the time in those around us. More than that, we are all part of one another's search. Through the simplicity, or lack of it, in our living, we help or hinder others in their search. The still waters of our heart can give clarity to others, while the disturbed waters muddy their way.

Moreover, as part of our search for direction, we often find ourselves as part of a religious tradition. This tradition speaks of generations of men and women who have found direction and have shared a common set of values which point out the direction we need to take. Though each person must initiate his or her own search in response to God's invitation, it is not necessary for each person to reinvent the wheel. The wisdom of the tradition is a precious gift which only the proud of heart would refuse to acknowledge.

These two aspects of our search are reflected in public and liturgical prayer. In public and liturgical prayer we acknowledge before one another that we share a common search for direction in life. We admit our total dependence on One who is beyond our power to control or manipulate. It is not enough to be simple and open before God. We must learn to bring these same qualities to all our dealings with one another, and shared prayer is a necessary part of this process.

In public and liturgical prayer I admit not only to God, but to my brothers and sisters, that I am in need of direction, that I fear losing my way, and that in fact, there are times when I have strayed. Through public prayer we create a common commitment to share with one another the ups and downs of our journeys, to be a strength and support for one another.

Liturgical prayer is a particular type of public prayer. It is the formal prayer of a particular religious community, expressing its faith in words, symbols and sacraments. By participating in liturgical prayer, I express my identification with a particular religious community, a Church, whose wisdom I treasure. Liturgical prayer is not just *my* prayer, it is the prayer of the community to which I belong. In liturgical prayer, words, symbols and actions come together to express the commonly held meanings and values which represent the profoundest insights, the tradition, of that community. Together, the community celebrates its common identity, its shared vision. It upholds and bears witness to the values which it proclaims as giving direction and meaning to human living. By participating in liturgical prayer, I immerse myself in these values as they are made present by word, symbol and sacrament. Such liturgical prayer is meant to celebrate and renew the life of the community by focusing attention on what it holds as most central.

For the Christian community, the focal point of our historical tradition is the person of Jesus Christ. In this person, who walked the countryside of Palestine nearly two thousand years ago, the Christian tradition finds someone who holds, and is held by, the mystery which is at the heart of life. The Christian tradition finds in Jesus one who is so immersed in the mystery of life that he not only shows us the direction, but has himself become that direction - 'I am the way' (John 14:6). Jesus not only shows us the direction, he show us the way to overcome all the forces which threaten to subvert our search, to turn us away from good and truncate our living. Thus, in his suffering unjustly at the hands of men, in his crucifixion, death and resurrection, Jesus reveals the power of self-sacrificing love to overcome evil and to give direction to our search.

In the Catholic tradition, this mystery of Jesus' suffering, death and resurrection is celebrated liturgically in the Eucharist, or as it is commonly called, the Mass. At Jesus' own request - 'Do this in remembrance of me.' (Luke 22:19) - the Catholic community gathers to recall the last fateful hours of Jesus' life, when he took bread and wine, blessed it and offered it to his disciples. Through his words and actions, a simple meal is transformed into the sign of a new covenant, a love-pact, through which the mystery of self-sacrificing love is symbolised. Catholic tradition sees the Eucharist as Jesus present again with his community, offering himself anew in self-giving love, to overcome the powers of darkness in our life and to provide sure guidance in our search for direction.

For the Catholic community, the celebration of the Eucharist is the central liturgical prayer. The Eucharist sums up the mystery at the heart of Christian belief. It celebrates the identity of the community which is formed in the living memory of Jesus, died yet risen. In the Eucharist, the Catholic community is called to travel the road that Jesus travelled, to imitate the mystery which it celebrates. As Jesus' heart was opened on the cross, so the Catholic heart must be opened anew, as it enters into the mystery of Jesus' death and resurrection. The Catholic heart formed in the Eucharist must be 'a magnanimous heart, an ecumenical heart, a heart capable of embracing the whole world' with its love. (Pope Paul VI, announcing the formation of the Secretariat for Non-Christians, Pentecost, 1966.)

Creed

For I handed on to you as of first importance what I in turn had received: that Christ died for our sins in accordance with the scriptures . . .

(I Cor. 15:3-4).

C

Catholic belief finds its most solemn expression in the recitation of the Creed in the Sunday Eucharistic gathering. Here, the whole community gathers and confesses its faith, that is, it states, as clearly and simply as possible, the truths and values which inform it in its search for meaning and direction.

The Creed is not a bare repetition of facts to which we assent. It is the distillation of the Church's wisdom and insight into the saving mystery of God's love as revealed in the death and resurrection of Jesus. It is like a compass to which we refer in our quest for direction and meaning.

The Creed did not simply drop out of the sky as a set of statements which God wants us to believe. It is the human product of centuries of argument which expresses what is central to Christian faith. From the very beginning, Christians have struggled to express their faith and to hand this on to succeeding generations. In his First Letter to the Corinthians, St Paul sought to hand on to the community a basic credal affirmation about the resurrection (I Cor. 15). Later, through solemn Church Councils, and as the result of often heated debate, a fuller statement of Christian faith was developed. The present Creed used in the Eucharist took on its present form at the Council of Constantinople (381 AD), though it is referred to as the Nicene Creed, from the Council of Nicea (325 AD). It has remained the basic statement of faith for most Christian communities throughout the world.

It is fitting that this central statement of faith is in the form of a liturgical prayer. As liturgical prayer, it both celebrates and forms the common identity, the shared meanings and values, of the community. As public prayer, it involves the recognition of ourselves as sharing a common humanity, a common search, with all our strengths and failings. As prayer, it is a still moment wherein we place ourselves before the mystery of God and humbly acknowledge our dependence upon Him. All this is part of praying the Creed:

We believe in one God,
the Father, the Almighty,
maker of heaven and earth,
of all that is, seen and unseen.

We believe in one Lord, Jesus Christ,
the only Son of God,
eternally begotten of the Father,
God from God, Light from Light,
true God from true God,
begotten, not made,
of one Being with the Father.
Through him all things were made.
For us men [and women] *and for our salvation*
he came down from heaven,
by the power of the Holy Spirit
he became incarnate from [was born of] *the Virgin Mary, and was made man* [became human].

For our sake he was crucified under Pontius Pilate;
he suffered death and was buried.
On the third day he rose again
in accordance with [in fulfilment of] *the Scriptures;*
he ascended into heaven
and is seated at the right hand of the Father.

He will come again in glory to judge the living and the dead,
and his Kingdom will have no end.
We believe in the Holy Spirit, the Lord, the giver of life,
who proceeds from the Father and the Son.
With the Father and the Son he is worshipped and glorified.
He has spoken through the prophets.
We believe in one holy catholic and apostolic Church.

We acknowledge one baptism for the forgiveness of sins.
We look for the resurrection of the dead,
and the life of the world to come. Amen.

We believe ...

The opening words of the Creed remind us that it is the prayer of a community. Faith is not my private possession. It is something which I share with others and have received from others, a common possession, a common gift. It is fitting then that we begin the Creed with an assertion, celebration and witness to our common faith - *we* believe.

in One God ... Father ... Son ... Holy Spirit

Immediately, our attention is turned to the mystery at the heart of life, the mystery we call God. In our belief in *God* we state our conviction that there is indeed a reality at the heart of life, that all our deepest longings for justice, for meaning, for purpose in living, are not pointing to an illusion. This conviction is not based on abstract philosophical reasoning, but arises from the lived experience of generations of Christians and others who have found direction and meaning.

Further, we assert that there is *one* God. While there may be many different searches, many different paths as found in the great religions of the world, our search has only one goal. While there are many pretenders who would claim our allegiance - the economy, the State, the club or political party - none of these can ever satisfy our deepest longings. None of these can demand our total commitment.

While Christians believe in *one God*, the Creed uses the term 'God' in relation to *three persons*: Father, Son and Holy Spirit. Here, Christian faith touches on a mystery which lies in the very heart of God. The oneness of God is not a unity without diversity, a unity which destroys difference. Rather, it is the unity of distinct persons in relationship, a unity in the giving and receiving of love. However, more than just being an obscure fact about God, this vision of God says something to us about the whole of reality. Since God is the source of all being, everything reflects something of God. Human societies reflect God's being when their communities are built upon a giving and receiving of love, when they do not destroy diversity simply because it is different, but nurture and respect it. In this way, the doctrine of *the Trinity* is telling us something about life itself. It is in mirroring the life of the Trinity that we find meaning, purpose and direction in our lives.

This doctrine of the Trinity is unique to Christian faith. It arises not from some abstract speculation about the divine nature, but from the lived experience of Jesus who received from the Father the fullness of the Spirit. Indeed, this is the continued experience of the Church. As human beings, we fall before the mystery at the heart of life, the God who is our Father. We come together in the living memory of Jesus the Son, who suffered, died and rose again. We are enlivened and empowered by the Spirit given to us, who speaks the unspoken prayers of our hearts. This is the Trinity of Christian faith.

... the Father, the Almighty, maker of heaven and earth, of all that is, seen and unseen

The Creed proclaims the God who is Father as *the Almighty* one, the source of all that is, *maker of heaven and earth.* This embraces everything, from the stars and galaxies, down to the tiniest sub-atomic particles. Our own planet in all its beauty and diversity, is but a part of God's handiwork, and human beings have a special place in God's creation. God has made us (women and men) in the divine image and likeness, giving us stewardship over the rest of creation. All this is the work of the God who is Father.

Moreover, the creative act is not some event lost in the distant past. The Father's creative activity is ongoing, creating and sustaining all things at all times. Thus, faith does not commit us to upholding or denying any particular scientific account of the universe and its development, be it the 'Big Bang', or the theory of evolution. Scientific problems demand scientific answers. Faith tells us not about the 'how' of creation, but about the 'why' of creation, its purpose and direction.

While the Creed speaks of the Father as the Almighty one, the might of God, the power of God, is not the power of a tyrant, who demands strict obedience under the threat of pain and death. No, the power of the Father is the overwhelming power of love, a love which is always able to overcome evil. At times, the almighty power of the Father will appear as the powerlessness of the suffering Jesus on the cross, a tragic victim of human evil. Yet, the power of God's love turns this evil around in the resurrection, so that even death is rendered powerless - 'Where, O death, is your sting?' (I Cor. 15:55).

As it is this Father who is the maker of heaven and earth, we believe that love is our origin, our purpose and our end. All things find their origin in the love of the Father. All creation is encompassed in his love. No part of creation, no matter how distorted by the power of evil, is beyond the Father's saving love. As such, the saving, provident love of the Father is the ground of our hope, a hope which need never despair. Thus this article rejects any notion of some evil being, equal to God in power, beyond God's provident reach. Even the 'evil one' is part of God's creation. Hence, his evil intentions are subject to ultimate frustration.

Indeed this article of the Creed reminds us that there are realities beyond our empirical world, that the Father is creator of 'all that is, seen *and unseen*'. While our vision of creation can never exclude the world of our senses - that which we can see and touch - it should not be limited to it. In particular, the dead remain as part of God's creation, even though they are no longer part of our everyday experience.

Finally, though the name 'Father' is given to God by Jesus - 'Abba, Father' (Mark 14:36) - this does not imply that somehow God is masculine rather than feminine. Indeed, an early Council of the Church (Toledo, 675 AD) spoke of the Son as being 'begotten or born out of the Father's *womb*'! God is beyond gender, God is both Father and Mother. While Father is a special name derived from Jesus' own usage, it does not limit us in the names we might give, out of our own prayer, to the Almighty One who is the source of all being, the One, who is without origin, yet from whom everything comes.

We believe in one Lord, Jesus Christ, the only Son of God, eternally begotten of the Father, God from God, Light from Light, true God from true God, begotten, not made, of one Being with the Father. Through him all things were made.

This article of the Creed represents the outcome of the most hard-fought battle of the early Church. It is the key issue over which the Council of Nicea was called. At its heart, lies the question of the identity of a Galilean carpenter turned wandering teacher, named Jesus. At issue is the relationship between Jesus and the God whom he called 'Abba, Father'. Is his relationship to God simply another instance of a relationship shared by all creation, or is it something unique and special?

The overwhelming answer given by the Council of Nicea is that this relationship is not simply another instance of the relationship shared by all creation. The relationship of intimacy which Jesus shared with the Father goes beyond that experienced by all others. Because of this special intimacy, Jesus not only speaks to us about the Father, he is the Father's special Word to us - 'whoever sees me sees the one who sent me' (John 12:45) - a Word which speaks of the Father's love and compassion.

To give expression to the relationship between the Father and Jesus, the Creed gives a torrent of words, an outpouring of faith - *eternally begotten of the Father, God from God, Light from Light, true God from true God, begotten, not made, of one Being with the Father* - all of which seek to express the uniqueness of that relationship. Because of his relationship to the Father, Jesus is not just another creature like us. He is God, Light, true God, of one being with the Father.

In the first instance, this article of faith demands a radical new understanding of the nature of God. It indicates the transition point from a Jewish monotheism to a Christian Trinitarian faith. The consequences of this we have already mentioned above.

In the second instance, it demands a radical new understanding of what it means to be human. The humanness of Jesus of Nazareth is not at issue. What it means, however, is that the barrier between the human and the divine has once and for all been broken. It is the human Jesus who is divine. In all its limitations and suffering, our humanness does not separate us from God. The only thing that can separate us from God is sin. Yet Jesus shows us that sinfulness is not part of human nature and that our humanity as such is nothing to be ashamed of. Indeed to be human is to be capable of God - God became human so that the human may become divine.

Christian faith, then, takes its stand on the unique relationship between Jesus who was born, matured, suffered, died and rose again, and the God he called 'Father'. There have, of course, been many other people who have experienced a special intimacy with the Source of all that is - the Buddha, Mohammed, Moses, Abraham, and the many Christian saints. While we can recognise the importance of each of these great teachers, Christian faith sees in Jesus an 'omega point' (to use de Chardin's phrase), something which marks, not just a quantitative, but a qualitative, difference. All these others may have spoken God's word to us, but Jesus *is* the Father's Word, the definitive revelation of what it means to be God and what it means to be human. Thus, in Jesus, Christians find the Way - 'I am the Way, the Truth and the Life' (John 14:6) - they find direction in life which leads to the Father. Jesus is the *one Lord, Jesus Christ, the only Son of God.*

For us men [and women] and for our salvation he came down from heaven

The previous article of the Creed speaks of the person of Jesus as *eternally begotten of the Father.* Here Christian faith believes that the relationship which defines the identity of Jesus is eternally established in God's own being. Even apart from creation, there is, in the mystery of God, the Son who is eternally begotten of the Father. It is this *eternally begotten* Son who *came down from heaven,* who takes on, and expresses himself in, the human life of Jesus of Nazareth.

Moreover, the purpose of Jesus' mission is not some idle curiosity, much less is it to receive praise and adulation from people. Rather, it is *for us and for our salvation* - 'The Son of Man came not to be served but to serve, and to give his life a ransom for many' (Mark 10:45). Jesus has a mission from the Father, a mission to give the Good News of the Father's love and compassion. He comes for our sake, because we are radically in need of this Good News.

This need we have is *for our salvation.* We know that in our search for direction and meaning, it is so easy to lose our direction, to see life as meaningless. Moreover, there are many forces at work which cloud our vision - the constant lure of a consumer society, the fears and anxieties which close us in upon ourselves, the false idols of pleasure and greed. These forces seek to break the bonds between us, to isolate and then destroy us by undermining our humanity. Rather than build a community of love, we risk reducing people to cogs in a machine, each an interchangeable part, to be used, worn out and replaced by another.

Thus, we see Jesus, in his mission, working for the sake of human salvation. Jesus reaches out to those whose humanity has been undermined through sickness, prejudice, religious legalism, and political and economic oppression. To those who are hungry, he offers the companionship of a shared meal, to those who are isolated, he offer real friendship and entry into his Father's kingdom. To the sick, he brings restored health, to the sinful he offers forgiveness from God. This is the salvation that Jesus offers, a salvation which can overcome every sadness, every injustice, every division between people.

This is not a salvation which simply offers consolation for present suffering with the hope of a future reward. It is a salvation which begins in the here and now, in the transformation of human relationships, working towards the creation of a community of love, a community which mirrors the dynamic love of the Trinity. This is the direction we seek, a direction which even death cannot undermine.

by the power of the Holy Spirit, he became incarnate from [was born of] the Virgin Mary

The Incarnation of the Son in the humanity of Jesus does not come about as the result of some purely natural process. It is not simply the high point of some natural evolutionary process leading on to ever higher forms of life. It comes about as a pure gift from God, *by the power of the Holy Spirit.* The clearest historical expression of this is that Jesus *became incarnate from* [was born of] *the Virgin Mary.* The Incarnation of the Son in the human Jesus is not the result of human activity, not some human achievement, but it is a powerful symbol of God's freedom and grace operating in human history. It reminds us that, in our search for direction, we must be ready to humbly accept God's own offer of assistance and not insist in pride on 'going it alone'.

In many ways, Mary epitomises this humble attitude, a willingness to participate in God's response to the human need for salvation. In her willingness to be the mother of Jesus, Mary freely gives her life over totally to partake in this divine response. In this regard, belief in Mary's *perpetual virginity* is not an anti-sexual sentiment. Rather, it sees Mary as a prototype for all those who, like her son, have 'made themselves eunuchs for the sake of the kingdom of heaven' (Matthew 19:12). Freely entered into, this is a powerful symbol of a total commitment to participation in God's response to the human need for salvation.

Because of her special place in the human story of salvation, Mary has been the centre of much reflection, prayer and gratitude within the Christian community. The Catholic Church, in particular, has reflected on Mary's origin and her end. Because of her special role, the Church has seen in Mary someone who, from her very beginning, has been free from all the distortions which mar and blur the human search for direction and meaning. In the doctrine of the *Immaculate Conception*, the Church proclaims Mary's freedom from original sin (see below for discussion on original sin). Here Mary is seen as the mature fruit of the seed planted in Abraham, our father in faith, fertilised by the Mosaic law and cultivated by the prophets. In her own person, Mary expresses all that is best in the Old Testament yet, at the same time, she is a bridge to the new covenant in her Son.

Similarly, in her death, the Church sees Mary as enjoying the same glorified state as her Son, Jesus. In the doctrine of the *Assumption*, the Church expresses its belief that Mary continues to enjoy a fully human existence, 'body and soul, assumed into heaven'. In expressing these beliefs, the Church does not separate Mary from the rest of humanity. Rather, it sees in Mary a 'sign of sure hope and solace'. In Mary, as in no other, we see the fullness of God's gift of salvation at work. In honouring Mary, Catholics are honouring the God who is at work in her life; seeing Mary, her good works, her values, her attitudes, we may 'give glory to [our] Father in heaven' (Matthew 5:16).

and was made man [became human*]

To the early followers of Jesus, his humanity was obvious. They saw in him a human being who had all the needs and limitations that they had. He slept and ate, cried and laughed, stubbed his toe, made friends. Most importantly, he prayed. However, as time moved on, there were those in the Church who began to focus more and more on Jesus' divinity. They neglected or idealised his humanity, turning it into something unreal, a shell or mask. The Councils of Nicea and Constantinople were not called to address this issue. It was not dealt with until the Council of Chalcedon (451 AD) which spoke of Jesus as being one person with two natures, human and divine. Thus, in the Creed, we have the simple statement that the Son *was made man* (i.e. became human). Clearly, it is the faith of the Church that Jesus is fully human - a thinking, feeling, bodily human being, with all the human limitations which this entails. There is nothing that is part of being human which Jesus does not share with us.

* The Greek term is derived from *anthropos*, which means 'human being', not a male.

However, while the humanity of Jesus was obvious to his early followers, something else was also clear. He 'in every respect has been tested as we are, yet without sin' (Hebrews 4:15). Jesus is like us in all things but sin. From this we learn two things. Firstly, the fact of our human limitations should not cause us to despair. Human limitation is not sinful so we need not feel guilty about it. Secondly, we cannot simply excuse our sinfulness with the line, 'Well, I'm only human.' There is nothing human about sin. Sin is losing our direction, or worse still, giving up the search. It undermines and distorts our humanity. Jesus was put to the test in exactly the same way we are, yet he never lost direction, never gave up the search.

For our sake he was crucified under Pontius Pilate

With this article of the Creed, we enter into the mystery of our salvation hard won through the death and resurrection of Jesus. It is for us and for our salvation that the Son became incarnate. It is for our sake that Jesus teaches us the power of self-sacrificing love to find and, indeed, to create meaning and direction in a world dominated by forces which seek to undermine our searching. It is Jesus' total love of the Father and his fidelity to his mission from the Father which leads to his being *crucified under Pontius Pilate*. This mention of Pilate is not incidental. It reminds us that our faith is grounded in historical events and persons, but the mention of Pilate also stands as a powerful symbol of all those who, through indifference, the misuse of power, and self-righteousness, crucify the poor and the weak, the hungry and the sick. These are the ones with whom Jesus identifies -' ... just as you did it to one of the least of these who are members of my family, you did it to me' (Matthew 25:40). It is through our attitudes and actions towards these whom Jesus especially loved that we can tell if we have lost our direction in life.

he suffered, died and was buried

There is nothing glorious in death on a cross. It is a slow and agonising death, from dehydration, exhaustion and eventual asphyxiation. Jesus enters fully into the human tragedy of death, facing it in all its ugliness. Yet it is this symbol, of Jesus nailed to the cross, which is the central focus in any Catholic Church. It is a constant reminder of the evil we can do, of taking the life of the innocent victim. It is a constant reminder that there are things to fear more than death. It is better to die than to turn away from our search for direction, to turn away from integrity, from honesty, from goodness.

Jesus was faced with the inevitability of his own death. It was not as if it was God's will that Jesus die violently on a cross. But Jesus knew that if he continued to do God's will, if he continued to reach out to the poor, the sinners, the sick, that he would meet with a violent end, as had John the Baptist before him. Given this awareness, Jesus sought to give his coming death a special meaning. Death does not simply overtake Jesus, catching him unawares. He faces death squarely, even embraces it, as he makes his death the sign of a new covenant, a love-pact which binds together his disciples within the coming reign of God.

Thus, on the night before he died, Jesus ritualised the events which were to occur. Through the symbolism of the breaking and sharing of bread, the pouring out and sharing of wine, and the washing of his disciples' feet, he sought to convey to them the meaning he gave to his coming death, a death which was the culmination of a life of self-sacrificing love, now to be poured out to establish a new covenant, for the forgiveness of sins. Jesus urges his disciples to continue his mission of self-sacrificing love - 'do this in remembrance of me' (Luke 22:19) - ritualised in a memorial of his passion, his suffering and death. This is the heart of the Eucharist.

On the third day he rose again, in accordance with [in fulfilment of] the Scriptures

If the death of Jesus were the end of the story, if that was all there was to say, we would be left with simply one more example of a sad and tragic history of violence against those who have identified themselves with the poor and suffering. Jesus would be remembered as a good man who met a sorry end. Yet the death of Jesus is not the end of the story. *On the third day he rose again*, raised up by the Father's love, breaking the bonds of death and entering into a new and glorious existence. In raising up Jesus, the Father reveals once and for all that love is more powerful than death and that He stands with Jesus on the side of the poor and suffering.

The nature of this glorious risen existence is beyond our imagining. It involves a continued, ongoing relationship with the material order, with human history. In the resurrection, Jesus remains an active agent in human history, through his Spirit, through his body, the Church, and in ways we cannot imagine. For Catholics, the most significant sign of this continued presence of Jesus in the world is in his eucharistic presence in the consecrated elements of bread and wine.

In stating that these events are *in fulfilment of the Scriptures*, the Creed is not asserting that somehow God wanted Jesus to die a horrible death on the cross. Rather, it is asserting that, despite the evil done by men and women, God's providential love is able to turn evil around, even the evil of Jesus' unjust crucifixion, and draw good from it. By referring to the Scriptures, the Creed reminds us that all these events have occurred within the framework of God's response to the human need for salvation. It reminds us that, in the end, God's victory over evil is assured.

he ascended into heaven and is seated at the right hand of the Father

It would, of course, be naive to take this article as asserting a literal fact. Heaven is not 'up' there for Jesus to 'ascend' into, nor does the Father have a right hand! We need to look deeper than that.

When the Scriptures speak of Jesus *seated at the right hand of the Father* (e.g. Romans 8:34, Hebrews 10:12), the image they have in mind is of ancient kings who would designate their heirs by seating them at their right hand. The heir would then share in all the authority and power of the king. In stating that Jesus is *ascended into heaven and seated at the right hand of the Father* the Creed asserts that Jesus, in his resurrected state, now shares fully in the power and authority of the Father. As the Risen Jesus states in Matthew's Gospel: 'All authority in heaven and on earth has been given to me' (Matthew 28:18). However, Jesus does not use this power and authority as did the self-serving rulers of the past (and the present). Rather, Jesus uses his position of influence to plead for us, to intercede with the Father on our behalf (Romans 8:34, Hebrews 7:25). Even in his risen life, Jesus continues to pour out his love for those in need. It is for this reason that St Paul can exclaim:

> *For I am convinced that neither death, nor life, nor angels, nor rulers, nor things present, nor things to come, nor powers, nor height, nor depth, nor anything else in all creation, will be able to separate us from the love of God in Christ Jesus our Lord* (Romans 8: 38–39).

With Jesus *seated at the right hand of the Father*, we can always approach God with confidence that our deepest yearnings can be met, that our deepest hurts can be healed, that our greatest hopes can be fulfilled.

He will come again in glory to judge the living and the dead, and his Kingdom will have no end.

Seated at the right hand of the Father, Jesus exercises the role of judge - 'the Father judges no one but has given all judgement to the Son' (John 5:22). Yet paradoxically, God sends his Son not to 'condemn the world, but in order that the world might be saved through him' (John 3:17). The judgement that Jesus brings to *the living and the dead* is not an extrinsic judgement, by some external judge. It is rather a judgement made by ourselves as we freely decide either to turn towards, or away from, God. Thus, in John's Gospel, Jesus proclaims:

> *And this is the judgment, that the light has come into the world, and people loved darkness rather than light because their deeds were evil. For all who do evil hate the light and do not come to the light, so that their deeds may not be exposed. But those who do what is true come to the light, so that it may be clearly seen that their deeds have been done in God* (John 3:19-21).

At a time of so many secretive and corrupt dealings at the highest level of our society, we see how true these words are.

Further, as Jesus comes *again in glory to judge*, he does not simply sit in judgement, he is also the standard by which we will all be judged. Jesus provides us with the perfect example of self-sacrificing love poured out so as to overcome evil. The consequences of this are spelt out for us in Matthew's Gospel, where Jesus is presented as describing the last judgement scene, Matthew 25:31-46. Here, Jesus gives us the criteria by which we are judged, whether we have fed the hungry, clothed the naked, visited the sick and imprisoned. This is not some list of 'religious' duties, but rather a sure compass in our search for direction and meaning in life. The criteria of our judgement is our generativity, our generosity, our commitment to justice and mercy for all. These criteria are evaluated through our simple human relationships with others, as expressed individually, socially and historically.

Of course, compared with the standard of Jesus we would all feel inadequate. Yet we can approach God in confidence, trusting in the divine mercy:

> *And by this we will know that we are from the truth and will reassure our hearts before him whenever our hearts condemn us; for God is greater than our hearts, and he knows everything. Beloved, if our hearts do not condemn us, we have boldness before God* (I John 3:19–21).

We believe in the Holy Spirit, the Lord, the giver of life, who proceeds from the Father and the Son. With the Father and the Son he is worshipped and glorified.

While the Holy Spirit is briefly mentioned with regard to the Incarnation, in this article of the Creed, we state more fully our belief *in the Holy Spirit*. The Spirit's work is not to be found in the majesty of creation, as with the Father, or in the historical existence of Jesus. Rather, the work of the Spirit is found in the inner movements of the human heart, drawing us to the Father, opening us to the Word, incarnate in Jesus. It is the Spirit who guides us from within, like the magnetism of the needle ensuring the compass points north-south. It is the Spirit who assists us in our prayer, interceding 'with sighs too deep for words' (Romans 8:26).

Thus, the Creed speaks of the Spirit as *the Lord, the giver of life*. Initially, this image is drawn from Genesis Chapter 2, where Yahweh, God, breathes his breath, his Spirit, into the man, Adam, to make him a living being (Genesis 2:7). However, the life that the Spirit gives is not merely a human existence, but much more. It is a share in the divine life itself (II Peter 1:4), a drawing in of human existence into the very dynamism of the Trinity. The life that the Spirit gives wells up within us to eternal life (John 4:14). All this is the work of the Holy Spirit.

Strange as it might seem, the next part of the Creed, which speaks of the Holy Spirit proceeding *from the Father and the Son*, is one of the most controversial parts of the Creed. The original Creed, promulgated at the Council of Constantinople originally stated that the Spirit proceeded *from the Father*. The Western (Catholic) Church, under the influence of the Trinitarian theology of St Augustine, began to add the phrase *and the Son* (referred to by the Latin term *filioque*), from about the eighth century. This exacerbated divisions between Eastern Orthodox Churches and the Western Catholic Church, which eventually ended in schism. The *filioque* clause is a matter of ongoing ecumenical dialogue.

At one level, however, the phrase, *proceeds from the Father and the Son*, is saying something very simple. The early disciples of Jesus sensed in him a powerful presence, a powerful spirit at work. Yet they knew that this was not a new spirit. The spirit of Jesus was not about overturning everything they had learned and valued from the Law and the prophets. The spirit of Jesus was none other than the Spirit who had spoken to the Hebrew people from of old, the same Spirit that Yahweh had sent to them to console and challenge them in their long and troubled history. Jesus 'speaks the words of God, for he gives the Spirit without measure' (John 3:34). The Holy Spirit is the Spirit of the Father and the Spirit of Jesus.

This article of the Creed also asserts the full equality of the Holy Spirit with the Father and the Son. *With the Father and the Son he is worshipped and glorified.* The Spirit is fully

God, just as the Father is fully God and the Son is fully God, and so the Spirit *is worshipped and glorified* in all our prayers and our actions of justice, mercy and love. With the Father and the Son, the Spirit constitutes the one God, the Trinity, whose life of dynamic love reveals to us the direction and meaning of our living.

He has spoken through the prophets.

As we noted above, the Spirit who was at work in Jesus is the same Spirit who *has spoken through the prophets* in the Old Testament. This same Spirit was at work in the many inspired authors of both the Old and New Testaments, which constitute the Christian Bible. The Catholic Church accepts seventy-three books as part of the Bible, twenty-seven being books of the New Testament (Protestants do not accept some Old Testament books as part of the Bible). The books of the Bible represent a variety of literary forms, from the myths of ancient peoples, to legends, poems and prayers, letters and historical narratives. All of these diverse books seek to give expression to the human search for meaning as it encountered the divine response to the human need for salvation, as experienced in the history of the Jewish people.

For Christians, the most sacred of these books are the *Gospels*, four books traditionally ascribed to Matthew, Mark, Luke and John. These books tell the story of Jesus, as he preached and loved, healed and suffered, as he died and rose again. They are not dispassionate, historical diaries seeking to give us every detail of this story. They are written by believers, for specific communities of believers, in order to build up their faith. They tell the true story of Jesus, by bringing out its deepest significance. In Jesus, they see the complete invitation issued to humanity to participate in the divine response to the human need for salvation. What they ask of us is faith. They challenge us to change, to repent and be converted.

In saying that the books of the Bible are *inspired*, we do not believe that these books are somehow the product of a divine dictation, with the authors acting merely as secretaries. The human authors of the Biblical books are true, human authors. They 'made full use of their powers and faculties' (*Verbum Dei*, n.12) - study, reflection, prayer, research, checking sources - to give expression to the faith of the Church. Inspiration is not a substitute for hard work. Indeed, it is only after the work is complete that the Christian community can stand back and say, 'This book truly presents our faith. It is truly inspired by the Holy Spirit.' In stating this, the Christian community has used words like *inerrancy* and *infallibility*. This does not mean that the Bible is without error in all matters, for example in matters of scientific or historical fact. It means rather that the Bible is a sure statement of our faith, and a sure revelation of God's response to the human need for salvation. Thus the Second Vatican Council taught that:

> *we must acknowledge that the books of Scripture, firmly, faithfully and without error, teach that truth which God, for the sake of our salvation, wished to see confided to the sacred Scriptures'* (*Verbum Dei*, n.12)

Since these book are truly the product of human authors, if we are to understand them correctly, we must have some appreciation of the human forms of communication which these authors use. Thus:

> *in determining the intention of the sacred writers, attention must be paid, inter alia, to 'literary forms for the fact is that truth is differently presented and expressed in the various types of historical writing, in prophetical and poetical texts', and in other form of literary expression* (ibid., n.12)

Thus, there is no place in the Catholic faith for a Biblical fundamentalism which ignores questions of literary form.

Finally, Catholics recognise that they do not have a controlling power over the Holy Spirit:

> *The wind blows where is chooses ... So it is with everyone who is born of the Spirit* (John 3:8).

The Spirit is not the sole possession of Catholics. It is also at work in other Christian communities and as well in non-Christian faiths. All who seek God with a sincere heart do so under the inner influence of the Spirit. This same Spirit has raised up prophets in a variety of cultures and times, prophets who have sought to articulate something about the mystery at the heart of life, about the human search for direction and meaning, about the human need for salvation. The great religions of the world, e.g. Hinduism, Buddhism, and Islam, are the historical outcome of these prophetic people. Of these and other religions, Vatican II stated:

> *The Catholic Church rejects nothing of what is true and holy in these religions. She has high regard for the manner of life and conduct, the precepts and doctrines which, although differing in many ways from her own teaching, nevertheless often reflect a ray of that truth which enlightens all people* (*Nostra Aetate*, no.2).

We believe in one holy catholic and apostolic Church.

Belief in the Church is not belief in an institution, with all its failing members, from the greatest to the least, a Church 'always in need of purification' (*Lumen Gentium*, no.8). No, 'when we say "in the holy Catholic Church", this must be understood as referring to our faith in the Holy Spirit, who sanctifies the Church' (St Thomas Aquinas, *Summa Theologiae*, II-II q.1, a.9 ad 5). Our belief is that the Holy Spirit will never desert the Church, not that the Church and its members will never fail the Holy Spirit! It is because of the abiding presence of the Holy Spirit that Catholics believe in the *infallible teaching office* of the Church. In peak moments in its life, the Church can teach with certainty, through the Pope and Church Councils, the truth of its faith. However, such an infallible teaching office presupposes and requires the *infallible believing Church*, so that 'the whole body of the faithful who have an anointing that comes from the holy one (cf. I John 2:20 and 27) cannot err in matters of belief ... when they manifest a universal consent in matters of faith and morals' (*Lumen Gentium*, no.12).

Those who are entrusted with the teaching office of the Church - Popes, bishops and priests - are also entrusted with the governance of the Church. The Church is a complex human society with many competing demands and interests making calls on its resources. It is the *pastoral* role of the hierarchy to attempt to order this complex human society for the good of all so that the Church may better fulfil her own mission in the world. It would be naive to think that those who have been entrusted with these offices have always carried them out wisely, that they have all been saints, that they have all been beyond criticism. They, like us all, are in constant need of God's mercy and grace in order to fulfil the office to which they have been called.

As was stated above, the Church has a mission. It is called to be a sacrament of Christ's abiding presence in the world, i.e. 'a sign and instrument ... of communion with God and of unity among all people' (*Lumen Gentium*, no.1). The Creed speaks of this mission in terms of the Church being *one holy catholic and apostolic*. These marks of the Church are not simply facts which can be checked by looking at the life of the Church. There are demands which are placed upon the Church if it is to be true to its mission. The Church must be *one* - '... that they may all be one. As you, Father, are in me and I am in you, may they also be in us ...' (John 17:21). The Church must be *holy*. All its structures, all its members must be committed to participating in the divine response to the human need for salvation as they search together for direction and meaning in life. The Church must be *catholic*, it must embrace all that is good in human cultures and societies. Finally, it must be *apostolic*. This has two meanings. Firstly, the Church must find its origins in the witness of the apostles and the communities they founded. It is the faithful bearer of the apostolic *tradition*, which includes the New Testament witness, but also includes the living faith of the early Church. Secondly, the Church is called to be apostolic in the present day, to spread the Good New about Jesus, the Christ, died and risen. To be apostolic is to evangelise, to share with others, as did the early Church, the saving message about Jesus.

As the sacrament of Christ's abiding presence in the world, the Church expresses its inner life in a number of particular Sacraments. These Sacraments have their origin in the mission and saving actions of Jesus. Traditionally, the Catholic Church has acknowledged seven Sacraments. These can be conveniently categorised as follows: sacraments of initiation - *Baptism, Confirmation* and *Eucharist*; sacraments of vocation - *Holy Orders, Marriage*; and sacraments of healing - *Reconciliation* and *Anointing of the sick*.

As the name implies, the Sacraments of initiation are concerned with the initiation of a person into the life of the Church. Traditionally, the three sacraments of Baptism, Confirmation and Eucharist were conferred in a single initiation ceremony. In Eastern Orthodox Churches, this is still the practice and it has been restored in the Western Catholic tradition in the Rite of Adult Initiation. For children, the rites remain distinct. *Baptism* is the primary sacrament of initiation (see below). *Confirmation* is an anointing which confirms the action and presence of the Holy Spirit in the life of the

Christian. *Eucharist* initiates the person into the saving mystery of Jesus' passion and death. As food for our spiritual journey, it alone of the three sacraments is constantly repeated in the life of the Christian.

The sacraments of vocation refer to states of living which are part of the Christian life. *Holy Orders* ordains the Christian as a ministerial leader of the Christian community. As ministerial leader, or *priest*, the ordained Christian is concerned with preaching the Gospel, with liturgical leadership of the community and with pastoral responsibility for the community. The *bishop* exercises these same responsibilities at the level of the diocese of the Church. In particular, bishops have a special responsibility to maintain the apostolic preaching of the Church. The bishop is also the minister of ordination for priesthood. Thus the priest is a helper to the bishop and works in union with the bishop. Recently, the Church has taken steps to restore the ordained ministry of permanent *deacon*. Part of the traditional ministry of the Church, the deacon assists the bishop in special works of service.

The Sacrament of *Marriage* is the most beautiful illustration of the human being touched by the divine. In marriage, the love of man and woman, a most natural element in the human search for direction and meaning, is taken up into the divine response to the human need for salvation. For the Christian, marriage is not simply a social contract between two persons. It becomes part of the saving mystery of life, an avenue for God's grace and blessing, an arena for God's judgement and mercy. In declaring marriage to be a sacrament, the Church reminds us yet again that our salvation is not to be found in some special category called 'religion'. No, it is to be found in the ordinary aspects of our daily living, in married and family love, in all its personal and social dimensions. Since the love of husband and wife is seen as symbolising the love of Christ for his Church, Catholic faith sees solemn sacramental marriage as a permanent reality, not capable of dissolution by the Church or the State. It does, however, recognise that some marriage unions, though appearing to conform to the laws of marriage, are lacking in some aspect and so grants annulments in such cases.

Christians, perhaps more than most, realise that the search for direction is fraught with difficulties. There are few for whom life is smooth sailing. All are in constant need of healing the hurts of failure and human limitation. This issue is addressed by the Sacraments of healing, *Reconciliation* and *Anointing of the sick.* The Sacrament of Reconciliation deals with the many times we lose direction, or worse still, give up the search for direction, in life. As such, this Sacrament makes effective for each person the divine response to the human need for salvation. It brings each person into direct contact with God's forgiveness and mercy, as made present by the leader of the Christian community, the priest. Like sin, the Sacrament of Reconciliation is not just a private matter. Sin, repentance and forgiveness are matters which affect the whole Christian community. Thus, the priest acts not only as God's representative, but also as the representative of the community. The communal nature of sin and forgiveness are highlighted in the second and third Rites of Reconciliation.

The other Sacrament of healing, the *Anointing of the sick*, addresses those times when we come face to face with human limitation in illness. Such times of physical and psychological distress present us with a great temptation to give up our search for direction and meaning. The distress of illness can easily cause us to lose hope, to declare that life is meaningless. At such times, the Anointing brings to the sick the prayers and love of the whole Christian community. It serves to remind the sick person that God has not deserted him/her, and that the healing power of Jesus is made present through the prayers and concern of the Christian community.

Both these Sacraments of healing are realisations of aspects of Jesus' own mission to the sick and to sinners. In his ministry Jesus brought healing to the whole person, body and soul. Jesus' miracles tell us of his power to bring physical and psychological healing, as well as forgiveness of sin. The Sacraments of healing are a sign of the Church's continuing fidelity to this aspect of Jesus' saving ministry.

We acknowledge one baptism for the forgiveness of sins.

Baptism is the primary Sacrament of initiation into the Christian community. The original rite, which involved full immersion in water, symbolised the new Christian's entry into the saving mystery of Jesus' death and resurrection:

> *Therefore we have been buried with him by baptism into death, so that, just as Christ was raised from the dead by the glory of the Father, so we too might walk in newness of life* (Romans 6:4).

Baptism establishes a new relationship between the new Christian and God, who is made present to the Christian by the believing community. It is the responsibility of the community to make present the forgiving love of God, so that Baptism is truly *for the forgiveness of sins*. Since God is always faithful to the promises made in Baptism, *we acknowledge* only *one baptism*.

Traditionally, Baptism is pronounced 'in the name of the Father, and of the Son, and of the Holy Spirit' (Matthew 28:19). Through entry into the Christian community, the newly baptised person is drawn deeply into the Trinitarian love of God. The dynamic life of giving and receiving love within the Christian community is a dim reflection of the inner life of God and it is in participating in this dynamic that we find direction and meaning in life.

Since the time of Augustine (4th-5th century), Baptism, especially infant Baptism, has been associated with *original sin.* Though often trivialised in popular imagination with images of snakes and apples, belief in original sin has a very serious intent. While not denying the beauty and blessing of the whole of God's creation, it asserts that, even from the very beginning of our human existence, we find our search for direction in life starting off on the wrong foot. Already we are pointing in the wrong direction and in danger of losing our way. Moreover, this situation is not brought about by some arbitrary decree of God, but arises from the sinfulness of others. We are affected deeply by the sinfulness of others so that our own vision is clouded. Using the language of myth, the Book of Genesis tell us that this has been part of the human condition from the very beginning, that even the first humans knew sin and so affected the search of others. St Paul put it this way:

> *Therefore, just as sin came into the world through one man, and death came through sin, and so death spread to all because all have sinned ...* (Romans 5:12).

Because of original sin and its consequences we all find ourselves in need of salvation. Catholics also believe that Mary has been saved by being preserved free from original sin (the *Immaculate Conception*), whereas we are saved through Baptism which overcomes the effects of original sin.

Apart from original sin, the Catholic faith also distinguishes between *mortal sin* and *venial sin.* Venial sins are those which do not involve a radical break in our relationship with God. They are a loss of direction in one who is still honestly searching, a momentary lapse which, if not attended to, could lead to further problems, but of itself is not a grave matter. Mortal sin, on the other hand, involves a radical break in relationship with God. It is not just losing direction, but a more serious giving up of the search. This denial of the search for direction and meaning can lead to cycles of despair, sexual promiscuity, violence, materialism and ecological irresponsibility as the sinner seeks to fill the void which cries out from within. Repentance from such sin will involve a radical conversion, a repudiation of past behaviour and the desire to adopt a new way of living. The Church teaches that mortal sins require sacramental Reconciliation for their forgiveness. Thus, the whole Christian community is involved in the act of forgiveness and in the loving support of the forgiven person.

The Scriptures also speak of 'the sin against the Holy Spirit' which cannot be forgiven (Mark 3:28–30). It seems that this refers to a final impenitence, a refusal to accept the forgiving love of God. God is willing to forgive any sin, but the sin which refuses forgiveness cannot be forgiven!

We look for the resurrection of the dead

Perhaps the greatest mystery of human living is the mystery of death. In the search for direction and meaning in life, nothing confronts us with a greater sense of absurdity than death, particularly the tragic death of the young. The prospect of death can seem to cast a shadow over our whole life, causing us to despair of ever finding meaning to our living. It is often said that modern society suppresses death in much the same way that the Victorian era suppressed sexuality.

Yet our Christian faith must cause us to rethink our attitude to death. Jesus' fidelity to his mission, which led to his death, tells us that there are some things to fear more than death itself. It is a far more fearful thing to give up the search for direction and meaning.

Do not fear those who kill the body but cannot kill the soul; rather fear him who can destroy both soul and body in hell (Matthew 10:28).

For those who want to save their life will lose it, and those who lose their life for my sake, and for the sake of the Gospel, will save it' (Mark 8:35).

The Christian vision contains a hope which is not extinguished by death. In the death and resurrection of Jesus, victory is won over the final enemy, death itself, so that St Paul can exclaim: 'Where, O Death, is your victory? Where, O Death, is your sting?' (I Corinthians 15:55).

The Creed expresses this hope in the acclamation, *We look for the resurrection of the dead.* For those who have been faithful, as Jesus was, to the search for direction and meaning in life, death has become a doorway to a new and glorious existence, a resurrected life. This resurrected life is beyond anything we could hope for or expect, much more than the 'immortality of the soul' envisaged by philosophers, much more than the shadowy life of the spirits found in Greek and early Hebrew literature. Resurrected life is a fully human life, granted out of the fullness of God's love, a life which does not leave behind our material universe, but transforms it as Jesus' own body was transformed in his resurrection. How this will come about we do not know. But our hope is grounded in our faith in the resurrection of Jesus:

'*... if Christ has not been raised, then our proclamation has been in vain and your faith has been in vain'* (I Corinthians 15:14).

... and the life of the world to come

Christian faith tells us nothing about the details of *the life of the world to come*. Poets and visionaries can fill our imaginations with all sorts of fanciful pictures, but these are of dubious value, often reflecting a limited theological understanding. Faith is much more sober in its vision. Death brings with it judgement, not an external judgement, but an inner summation of our total life's search. Our fidelity to that search determines, in the light of God's mercy, the continued state of our existence.

Catholic faith speaks of three states of existence after death. It speaks of *purgatory*, a state of final purification. In some sense, death is not the end of human growth. In death, human persons must still confront the many faults and failings which have marred their living. Such a confrontation is painful, but it is the pain of growth. This is as we experience it in this life and we need not think that death will change this fact! However, it is pain mixed with joy, for the final goal is in sight. It is further part of Catholic faith that the healing of purgatory involves those who remain in this life and that prayer for the dead can be part of this healing process.

The final goal of human existence is eternal life with the Triune God - Father, Son and Spirit. This is *heaven*, to see God face to face (I Corinthians 13:12), to be one with our brothers and sisters who have shared our vision, who have found direction and meaning in our common journey. Scripture speaks of heaven as a wedding banquet (Luke 14:15f.), as a new city (Revelation 21:9f.), as a homecoming to the Father's mansion (John 14:1f.). All these images seek to convey something of the excitement of heaven. To be in heaven is to embrace, and be embraced by, the mystery at the heart of life, a mutual and eternal embrace which takes in the whole cosmos. While our imaginations constantly fail us in our attempts to envisage what heaven will be like, our hearts carry us forward with their longings, in a certain hope of what is to come.

While heaven is the final goal of human existence, it is not a goal which is achieved by some automatic process, a goal of some evolutionary process where the end is somehow guaranteed. The work of God's salvation always protects the dignity of our freedom, always seeks to enlist that freedom. The sad experience of human living is that people can refuse to participate in the divine response to our human need for salvation. They can turn away from the search for direction and meaning. When the Church speaks of *hell* it speaks a warning to us of the possibility that such a refusal may be permanent, that we may, in a final act of freedom, turn our back on God. The doctrine of hell reminds us of the seriousness of our search, of the importance of not giving up. Whether this possibility of final impenitence is ever realised, we do not know. Even the great mystic of the Church, St Therese of Lisieux could say, 'I believe in hell, but I think that it is empty'!

Amen.

The Creed concludes with the solemn affirmation by the community of all that the Creed contains. To say, 'Amen' is to say 'Yes, I give my living assent to all that has been said.'

Action

And what does the Lord require of you but to do justice, and to love kindness, and to walk humbly with your God.

(Micah 6:8)

Christian and Catholic faith brings with it not only joy and peace, but also a sense of responsibility. The problems of human living are not solved simply because one has found an initial direction in one's life search. There is a continuing demand for discipline and self-control as well as a continuing need for openness to the surprises which are ever present as we respond to the divine initiative.

However, while there are demands which flow from our response to God's invitation, the Christian is profoundly aware that these demands can only be met with the continued assistance of God's grace and support. There are no grounds for self-righteousness or self-adulation or self-congratulation in the Christian life. Christians are humbly aware that everything they have comes from God, that every good deed they do is made possible by God's grace. As St Augustine wrote in his *Confessions*, 'Command what you wish, but give what you command'! This is not a denial of human freedom. Rather, it is a profound realisation of the fragility of freedom, of our sinfulness which distorts freedom, and of our need for God's grace to enable our freedom. The starting point for the Christian's response to the demands of the world is prayer. It is in prayer that we touch the mystery at the heart of life which secures our freedom to do what is right.

The realisation of our dependence on God is not however a cause for timidity or inaction. The demands of the world are pressing and the wisdom of the Christian tradition give clear guidelines as to the type of response we are called to make. We are all called to respond as best we can.

Evangelisation

Go therefore and make disciples of all nations; baptising them in the name of the Father, and of the Son and of the Holy Spirit, and teaching them to obey everything that I have commanded you (Matthew 28:19-20).

Finding Christian faith involves a strong sense that faith is significant not only for oneself as an individual, but also for a world which so often seems to have lost its direction, a world which so often finds human living meaningless. Christian faith is not just a gift to treasure, it is a gift to share with others. The Christian believes that the life, death and resurrection of Jesus is a definitive response by God to the human need for salvation. Thus it has a significance for all people, at all times, as they search for direction in life.

The Christian life is always an invitation to others to enter, with those who live it, into the dynamic life of giving and receiving love as found in the Trinity. Hence it is in the name of the Trinity that Christians are baptised. Christianity offers the world a way of living, of relating, which can turn around the effects of evil and give meaning to life.

To evangelise does not mean standing on a street corner preaching from the Bible. Rather, it involves the constant invitation made by Christians who live in a new and different way from the ways of the world. All are called to give witness to family and friends through the quality of their living. Some will be called upon to give an explicit account of their faith in Jesus.

Whatever form it takes, evangelisation seeks to convert, not just individuals, but also social and cultural structures, towards truly human and sacred values. Thus, in his apostolic exhortation on evangelisation in the world, *Evangelii Nuntiandi*, Pope Paul VI proclaimed:

the Church evangelises when she seeks to convert, solely through the divine power of the Message she proclaims, both the personal and collective consciences of people, the activities in which they engage, and the lives and the concrete milieux which are theirs (para. 18).

Further, he spoke of this process of conversion as:

affecting and as it were upsetting, through the power of the Gospel, humankind's criteria of judgement, determining values, points of interest, lines of thought, sources of inspiration and models of life, which are in contrast with the Word of God and the plan of salvation (para. 19).

It is for this reason that Paul VI went on to say:

even the finest witness will prove ineffective in the long run if it is not explained, justified ... and made explicit by a clear and unequivocal proclamation of the Lord Jesus (para. 22).

Justice

One of the clear signs that human beings have lost direction is the extent of injustice present in the world. The media regularly inform us of poverty and suffering in Third World countries which stand in strong contrast to the affluence of First World countries. While millions lack basic food, shelter, fresh water and medicines, rich nations spend billions of dollars on arms and frivolous consumer items. This is far from the ideal which Christian faith reveals, a world community based on the giving and receiving of love. St John might well have been writing for us today when he said:

How does God's love abide in anyone who has the world's goods and sees a brother or sister in need and yet refuses help? Little children, let us love, not in word or speech, but in truth and action (I John 3:17–18).

In our present day these words have a compelling urgency. Some, even some Christians, have quoted the words of Jesus - 'you have the poor with you always' (John 12:8) - as if the plight of the poor is not a concern for Christians. Yet Jesus is referring to a verse from the Old Testament, with which his hearers would have been familiar:

> *Since there will never cease to be some in need on the earth, I therefore command you, 'Open your hand to the poor and needy neighbour in your land'* (Deuteronomy 15:11).

Rather than accepting the existence of the poor, Jesus is urging us all to greater generosity.

There is a growing awareness within the Church today that the demand of justice for the poor is not an added extra to Christian living. Many are beginning to see it as central to Christian faith. The Church in Latin America has coined the phrase 'preferential option for the poor', a phrase which has been picked up and echoed by Pope John Paul II. Our Christian faith calls on us not only to be aware and responsive to the needs of the poor, but to see the world through their eyes. They are not asking for charity, doled out from the surplus wealth of the rich. They are asking for justice, for a just price for their goods, just wages for their labour, and freedom from dictatorial political regimes propped up by Western countries. To meet such demands will require a re-visioning of our economic structures and our social and political values.

Such activities are part of the process of preaching the Gospel to the world. That is why Pope Paul VI spoke of the Gospel as converting 'both the personal and collective consciences of people', i.e. converting us not just at the individual level, but also at the collective level of our economic, social and political life. Thus, when the Synod of Bishops from around the world met in 1971 to discuss the problems of injustice in the world they stated:

Action on behalf of justice and participation in the transformation of the world fully appear to us as a constitutive dimension of the preaching of the Gospel, or in other words, of the Church's mission for the redemption of the human race and its liberation from every oppressive situation (Justice in the World).

Moral living

Apart from the specific demands generated by our response to the Gospel, Christians, like all people, are also called to act in a morally upright manner. Both the Bible and human wisdom are aware of the many ways in which we can lose our direction in life, the many ways in which we can sell ourselves short. Moral living demands a continual commitment to seeking the right response to any particular situation.

Conscience

The first principle of moral living is the human conscience. The Second Vatican Council spoke of conscience in the following terms:

Deep within his conscience man discovers a law which he has not laid upon himself, but which he must obey. Its voice, ever calling him to love and to do what is good and to avoid evil, tells him inwardly at the right moment: do this, shun that. For man has in his heart a law inscribed by God. His dignity lies in observing this law, and by it he will be judged. His conscience is man's most secret core, and his sanctuary. There he is alone with God, whose voice echoes in his depths (Gaudium et Spes, n.16).

As the Council indicates, human conscience and the freedom it generates are essential to human dignity. It is within conscience that we discover our moral identity. It is through our conscience that we are guided to moral action. It is through the decisions of our conscience that we shall be judged. Conscience is our sanctuary, which no one has the right to violate, for there we are alone with God.

The Church also recognises that conscience needs to grow and develop. The conscience of a child is not adequate to the moral decisions that need to be made by an adult. Conscience must be informed, by human experience and intelligence, by the wisdom of the past, by the values of the community and so on. As a person grows and encounters new experiences, new challenges, they can develop a greater moral sensitivity, a heightened conscience. This formation of conscience is a major responsibility for each person to undertake. Often we only learn from our mistakes which can be very painful, but confidence in God's mercy and forgiveness means that such mistakes are not the last word. We can begin again, perhaps a bit wiser, with a clean slate.

Church moral teaching

While conscience is intensely personal, that does not mean that it is isolated or without guidance. As with many areas of human living, mature persons will seek the advice of others in moral matters so as to draw on a wisdom which may be greater than their own. Such advice can have a detachment from our particular circumstances which allows us to see the moral situation more objectively. In this regard, all Christians see the Bible as a source of moral wisdom which can guide their living. Catholics also see the Church's traditional moral teachings and the present living voice of the Church's magisterium (i.e. teaching office) as a source of moral wisdom and authority.

Catholics see the Church's wisdom and authority as having a more than human source. They see the Church as guided by the inspiration of the Holy Spirit. Because of this inspiration:

> *the faithful ... are obliged to submit to their bishops' decision, made in the name of Christ, in matters of faith and morals, and to adhere to it with a ready and respectful allegiance of mind. This loyal submission of the will and intellect must be given, in a special way to the authentic teaching authority of the Roman Pontiff* [i.e. the Pope] (Lumen Gentium n.25).

This obligation is not opposed to conscience, but arises out of Catholic conscience which recognises its own limitations together with the wisdom and authority of the Church. On the other hand, neither can Church teaching be a substitute for conscience. No person can abdicate his/her moral responsibility to someone else and just 'do what he/she is told to do'. God does not want us to be moral robots, automatically obedient to the Church, without thoughtful reflection on our own part. Such automatic obedience would seriously erode human dignity. Human dignity lies in following the law of conscience, which is primary.

Finally, in the modern world there are many problems which have never confronted us before - over-population, pollution, nuclear weapons, unfair global trade, new medical technologies. The teaching office of the Church has no instant answers to these many problems and the moral dilemmas they cause. It can draw on moral principles from the past, but it is not always clear how the principles apply or whether they are adequate to the task. In many cases, the magisterium advises caution as it struggles to find answers. At such times, it is not just the magisterium, but all Catholics, indeed all people of good will, who must engage in the hard task of moral reflection, in seeking direction and meaning in the complexities of the modern world. At such times no one has a monopoly on wisdom or the Holy Spirit and all are called upon to contribute.

The Commandments

Moral wisdom has often been crystallised into collections of rules or commandments which express in summary form aspects of moral living. When approached by people in his own time Jesus gave one such summary:

> *'You shall love the Lord your God with all your heart, and with all your soul, and with all your mind.' This is the greatest and first commandment. And a second is like it: 'You shall love your neighbour as yourself.' On these two commandments hang all the law, and the prophets* (Matthew 22:37–39).

For Jesus, this 'command' to love is the heart of all moral and religious living - to love God, to love one's neighbour and to love oneself as loved into being by God. All our human and Christian responsibilities are summed up in love. Moreover, the love that Jesus has in mind is not a romantic feeling, but a practical heartfelt concern for others. When asked what it means to love our neighbour, Jesus gave us the magnificent parable of the Good Samaritan (Luke 10:29–37), a simple picture of practical neighbourly love.

Another well-known collection of commandments, which comes from the Old Testament, is the Ten Commandments. In their original setting these commandments established a covenant between Yahweh (God) and the Chosen People. The ten commandments set out the basic laws regulating the people's relationship to God and to one another. Historically, these laws established the Chosen People as a new society under the rule of Yahweh (God), much as a constitution establishes a modern State.

Now we tend to view the ten commandments, particularly the last seven commandments, as a summary of moral living. Indeed, many people around the world have similar sets of commandments which regulate human relationship in society.

A full account of the giving of the commandments in their historical context is found in Exodus 20:1–17. A concise list of the ten commandments is usually given as follows:

1. You shall honour no other god but me.
2. You shall not use the name of God in vain.
3. Keep holy the Sabbath day.
4. Honour your father and mother.
5. You shall not kill.
6. You shall not commit adultery.
7. You shall not steal.
8. You shall not bear false witness against your neighbour.
9. You shall not covet your neighbour's wife.
10. You shall not covet your neighbour's goods.

While these commandments are important and basic, they should not be seen as complete. They simply do not cover many moral questions faced in a complex modern society, e.g. Is it moral to minimise, or even avoid, paying taxes? Should I buy locally manufactured goods to help the local economy or imported goods from third world countries which are cheaper? What are my moral obligations regarding recycling and the use of non-biodegradable products? Is there a moral obligation to minimise the use of my car and make more use of public transport? The Ten Commandments will not give us answers to such questions. Yet these are the sorts of moral questions we face every day.

The Beatitudes

Moral living consists of more than obedience to a series of commands. Christians strive not only to fulfil their moral obligations, but to do so in a manner which reflects the very Spirit of Jesus. Often this will mean going beyond the letter of the law and 'going the extra mile'. Thus Jesus urges us not only to refrain from striking those who strike us, but to turn the other cheek (Matthew 5:38–42). It is not enough that we do not commit adultery, we must banish lustful thoughts as well (Matthew 5:27–30). In the Sermon on the Mount (Matthew 5–7), Jesus presents us with a new and higher 'law', or, more correctly, reveals what is possible with the help of his Spirit.

At the very beginning of this Sermon, Jesus gives us the Beatitudes. For the Christian, they are a much more important statement than the Ten Commandments since they give the basic spirit with which all commandments are to be carried out. They are concerned with attitudes rather than particular actions. These attitudes are to inform our whole search for direction and meaning. They are as follows:

Blessed are the poor in spirit, for theirs is the kingdom of heaven.
Blessed are those who mourn, for they will be comforted.
Blessed are the meek, for they will inherit the earth.
Blessed are those who hunger and thirst for righteousness, for they will be filled.
Blessed are the merciful, for they will receive mercy.
Blessed are the pure in heart, for they will see God.
Blessed are the peacemakers, for they will be called children of God.
Blessed are those who are persecuted for righteousness' sake, for theirs is the kingdom of heaven (Matthew 5:3–10).

The Beatitudes do not represent some form of 'optional extra' for Christians. Rather, they express something of the heart of Christian living, an ideal for which we are all called to strive.

Reconciliation

Christians, perhaps more than most, are aware that they do not live up to the ideals of the Christian life; indeed, as often as not they are guilty of serious moral failure. Christians make no pretence about being perfect. However, what Christians also know is the love and forgiveness of God. Without this love and forgiveness, our lives would be trapped in guilt and self-recrimination. Each of us would become 'a slave to sin', as St Paul puts it (Romans 6:17), unable to free ourselves from the compulsive power of sin, be it the compulsiveness of sexual promiscuity, of violence, or some of the more acceptable compulsions of our consumer society.

For Catholics, the usual means of experiencing forgiveness for our sins is through the Sacrament of Reconciliation. In this Sacrament, the forgiveness of God is made present so that, freed from the burden of our sins, we can get on with living as God wants us to. The Sacrament of Reconciliation thus has an important role to play in moral living.

However, this is only part of the story. As we were taught to pray in the Lord's Prayer:

Forgive us our trespasses,
as we forgive those who trespass against us

We cannot expect more from God's forgiveness than we are willing to give to others. This is a message emphasised in the parable of the unforgiving debtor (Matthew 18:23-35). Forgiveness of others is an important part of Christian living. To measure its importance, we need only consider the many societies which are at present being torn apart by hate and violence. (Indeed it is scandalous that some of these societies in fact call themselves Christian.) Without forgiveness, resentment at injustices fester into hatred, quickly taking people, and even whole societies, down a spiral of violence and destruction.

Jesus often emphasised the importance of forgiveness. From the cross, he spoke words of forgiveness to those who had crucified him. After his resurrection, he said to his disciples:

> *'Receive the Holy Spirit. If you forgive the sins of any, they are forgiven them; if you retain the sins of any, they are retained'* (John 20:22–23).

Where we fail to forgive, where we retain the sins of others, then they can be trapped in their sin. When we forgive others, then the words of the Beatitude are spoken to us: 'Blessed are the merciful, for they will receive mercy.'

Particular Moral Issues

Through various means, e.g. the documents of the Second Vatican Council, various encyclicals (papal letters), and the tireless labours of her moral theologians, the Church has built up a body of teachings on a variety of moral issues which affect contemporary Catholics. It is the responsibility of every Catholic to try to be informed about the content of these teachings and the issues they deal with. The following brief statements are only meant to give some of the flavour of these teachings.

Justice

For over one hundred years the Church has spoken out on issues of social justice - the right to form unions, the right to receive a just wage, the immorality of exploiting poorer nations, of political and cultural imperialism, of unjust trade and so on. Consistent throughout all this teaching has been a perspective which sides with the poor, the weak, the disadvantaged. As part of this teaching, the Church has condemned both communism and capitalism as political systems which exploit the weak and undermine social justice.

The Church also upholds the right to private property, but does not see this as absolute. The poor thus have some moral claim on the wealth of the rich, since the goods of the earth are meant for all people. The Church rejects both a collectivism which sees all property as belonging to the State and liberal capitalism which sees the right to private property as absolute.

Recently, the Church recognised the positive values of democratic systems as befitting human dignity and has opposed all forms of oppressive, totalitarian governments. While so opposed, it does not, in general, condone the use of violence in the overthrow of unjust governments, except as a last resort.

Many of these themes and more are taken up in the recent encyclical of Pope John Paul II, *Centesimus Annus*, which marked the centenary of *Rerum Novarum*, the first major encyclical on social justice which was issued by Pope Leo XIII in May 1891.

Peace

Since World War II and with the advent of nuclear weapons, the Church has consistently opposed the use of force to resolve international conflicts. In particular, the Church has condemned the use of weapons which kill indiscriminately such as nuclear weapons, or the mass bombing of civilian populations. While the Church has a traditional teaching on a 'just war', the conditions for such a war are quite limited and also impose conditions on the fighting of wars. Even when a war is seen as justified, it is seen as the lesser of two evils, never as a desirable course of action.

The Church has also condemned the arms race and the international trade in weapons. It sees the arms race as diverting resources from the urgent task of improving the living conditions of the poor. Pope John Paul II has called on the richer nations of the world to say, 'No' to the lucrative arms trade.

The Church has also supported the effort of bodies such as the United Nations since it clearly recognises the need for international solutions to conflict between nations. Ultimately the Church sees international conflict arising from injustices between nations. Thus peace can only come about through the pursuit of international justice. As Pope Paul VI once said, 'If you want peace, work for justice.'

Sexuality

While the Church's teaching in the area of sexual ethics receives much publicity, it is in fact little understood in our society. Present-day society tends to see sex as a recreational pastime between consenting adults. This attitude does nothing to shed light on the deep and powerful currents present in human sexuality. When these currents are not respected, we see consequences which are depressingly familiar - sexual violence, pornography, promiscuity, the destruction of relationships, and so on.

The Church, on the other hand, sees sexuality as part of a person's human identity. God has created us male and female (Genesis 1:27). When we express ourselves sexually, we are saying something from our whole person, not just engaging in recreation. The Church seeks to protect the dignity of human sexuality by maintaining that full sexual expression in intercourse is only valid within a committed married relationship.

Furthermore, the Church teaches that there is an intrinsic link between sexual expression and procreation. The Church teaches that each act of intercourse must be open to the possibility of conception, and so it rejects the use of artificial means of contraception. This teaching is the subject of continued debate within the Church.

Based on Biblical teaching and the intrinsic connection between sexual expression and procreation, the Church also sees homosexual sexual expression as morally disordered.

Recently, Biblical scholars have questioned whether Biblical injunctions against homosexual activity are against homosexuality itself or are against its association with pagan religious practices.

Medical Ethics

Advances in medical technology have brought a number of issues into prominence in modern times. Many of these issues raise complex moral questions, which the Church is called upon to investigate so as to advise and guide its members.

Perhaps the most prominent issue on which the Church has spoken out is that of abortion. The Church sees human life as sacred from the first moment of conception and, consequently, sees abortion as immoral. This is in harmony with the Church's mission of being a voice for the voiceless. However, it is also part of the Church's mission to bring the mercy and forgiveness of God to those who through human weakness and the pressure of circumstances may have lapsed in this matter. While abortion is seen as a serious matter it is not seen as being beyond God's forgiveness.

Another issue which has received attention from the Church in recent times is IVF (in vitro fertilisation or so-called 'test-tube babies') and associated technologies. The Church has approached these matters with extreme caution. At the level of moral theory, the Church questions the separation of intercourse from procreation which these technologies involve. At the practical level, there are many issues which remain unresolved - the experimental nature of the procedure, the fate of 'surplus' embryos, experimentation on embryos, legal questions, and so on. At the present time, the Church does not see these technologies as offering a morally acceptable solution to the problem of childless couples.

Finally, medical advances have raised many questions about prolonging human life in cases of terminal illness. While the Church opposes active euthanasia, it also argues that patients are not required to undergo extraordinary or experimental treatments to prolong life. The Church, for example, is not necessarily opposed to situations such as the turning off of respirators for terminally ill patients. In such matters, Church teaching is often more advanced than civil legislation.

Church moralists are also engaged in ongoing debate and discussion on issues such as the AIDS crisis, the just allocation of medical resources, the need for proper care of those in caring professions, and the place of Church moral stances in a pluralist society. There are no easy answers to these questions. Catholics should not expect the Church to provide immediate answers in every case of moral debate. Still, they can expect the Church to treat such issues seriously and to work towards greater clarity.

Environmental issues

A number of Church documents have made passing reference to the problems of the global environment. Recently, Pope John Paul II has issued a message to mark the World Day of Peace (1 January 1990) which took ecological concern as its theme. In it he noted that there is a new ecological awareness emerging which 'ought to be encouraged to develop into concrete programs and initiatives'. Further, he emphasises that *'the ecological crisis is a moral issue'* and that it 'has assumed such proportions as to be the *responsibility of everyone*'.

It should be noted that this is an area which has not received much attention in the past, but which is drawing more and more attention from the Church at all levels, from the official magisterium to the local parish community.

Church membership

As with any social group, membership of the Church brings with it both rights and responsibilities. Any social group must have its own structure and ways of organising its members in order to further its aims. Recently, the Church promulgated its revised code of Canon Law, which spells out in detail the various rights and responsibilities of members of the Catholic Church.

Without going into the detail of this code, the general obligations of a Church member are as follows: to participate in the life of the Church through celebration of the Eucharist on Sundays and designated Holy Days, through participation in the sacraments (Eucharist and Reconciliation at least once a year), by supporting the life of the Church financially where possible, studying Church teaching, observing the Church's marriage laws, bringing up one's children in the faith, and so on.

These responsibilities are usually spelt out in the form of human laws and minimum requirements. They may vary in their particulars from time to time and place to place. For further details, it is best to consult with the local parish priest.

Appendix

SOME PRAYERS

This is simply a collection of prayers from the rich Christian heritage.

The Lord's Prayer

Our Father, who art in heaven,
hallowed be thy name;
Thy kingdom come;
Thy will be done on earth as it is in heaven.
Give us this day our daily bread;
and forgive us our trespasses
as we forgive those who trespass against us;
and lead us not into temptation,
but deliver us from evil. Amen.

Hail Mary

Hail Mary, full of grace, the Lord is with you.
Blessed are you among women and blessed is the fruit of your womb Jesus.
Holy Mary, Mother of God, pray for us sinners, now and at the hour of our death. Amen.

Doxology (Glory be)

Glory be to the Father, and to the Son,
and to the Holy Spirit:
as it was in the beginning, is now and ever shall be,
world without end. Amen.

Magnificat

My soul proclaims the greatness of the Lord,
my spirit rejoices in God, my Saviour;
for he has looked with favour on his lowly servant,
and from this day all generations will call me blessed.

The Almighty has done great things for me:
holy is his name.
He has mercy on those who fear him
in every generation.

He has shown the strength of his arm,
he has scattered the proud in their conceit.
He has cast down the mighty from their thrones,
and has lifted up the lowly.
He has filled the hungry with good things,
and has sent the rich away empty.

He has come to the help of his servant Israel
for he has remembered his promise of mercy,
the promise he made to our fathers,
to Abraham and his children for ever.

Psalm 23

The Lord is my shepherd, I shall not want.
He makes me lie down in green pastures;
He leads me besides still waters;
he restores my soul.
He leads me in right paths
for his name's sake.

Even were I to walk throught the darkest valley,
I fear no evil, for you are with me.
Your rod and your staff - they comfort me.

You prepare a table before me
  in the presence of my enemies;
You anoint my head with oil;
  my cup overflows.

Surely goodness and mercy shall follow me
  all the days of my life.
And I shall dwell in the house of the Lord
  my whole life long.

Peace Prayer of St Francis of Assisi

Lord make me an instrument of your peace:
  where there is hatred, let me sow love;
  where there is injury, pardon;
  where there is discord, unity;
  where there is doubt, faith;
  where there is error, truth;

where there is despair, hope;
where there is darkness, light;
and where there is sadness, joy.

O Divine Master, grant that I may not so much seek
to be consoled as to console,
to be understood as to understand,
to be loved as to love.

For it is in giving that we receive
it is in pardoning that we are pardoned,
and it is in dying that we are born to eternal life.

Prayer of St Ignatius Loyola

Lord, I freely yield all my freedom to you.
Take my memory, my intellect and my entire will.
You have given me everything I am or have;
I give it all back to you to stand under your will alone.
Your love and your grace are enough for me;
I shall ask for nothing more.

Prayer of Mother Teresa Of Calcutta

Make us worthy, Lord,
To serve our fellow human beings throughout the world
who live and die in poverty and hunger.
Give them through our hands this day their daily bread,
And by our understanding love,
give peace and joy.

Prayer of John Henry Newman

Lead, kindly light, amid the encircling gloom,
Lead thou me on;
The night is dark, and I am far from home,
Lead thou me on.
Keep thou my feet; I do not ask to see
The distant scene; one step enough for me.

I was not ever thus, not prayed that thou
Shouldst lead me on;
I loved to choose and see my path; but now

Lead thou me on.
I loved the garish day, and, spite of fears,
Pride ruled my will: remember not past years.

So long thy power has blest me, sure it still
Will lead me on
O'er moor and fen, o'er crag and torrent, till
The night is gone,
And with the morn those Angel faces smile,
Which I have loved long since, and lost awhile.

INDEX